The Welcoming Table

The author has made every effort to ensure the accuracy of the information within this book was correct at time of publication.

For requests, information, and more contact Bruce D. Thornton at pppmy1stbook@gmail.com.

Available in ebook and print.

Print ISBN: 978-1-944643-32-4
LCCN: 2020922013

Cover designer: LaCricia A'ngelle

The Welcoming Table

BRUCE D THORNTON

HIS PEN
PUBLISHING LLC
Jeremiah 30:2

www.hispenpublishing.com

Acknowledgements

My mother use to say, "show yourself as friendly." This is the bases of my second book of poetry entitled, The Welcoming Table. Moreover, there is a particular biblical scripture that sum up the true essence and theme of this project. When the psalmist, David, in the 23:5 of his book of Psalms reads, **"Thou prepares a table before me in the presence of mine enemies."** The message is a clarion cry to make myself as a base so that I can be exalted later.

In the poem, **The Welcoming Table,** there is a line that say, *Come, set down at my expense and feast.* This is emblematic of killing folks with the kindness you're offering them when they are purposefully trying to do you harm. It's God promise that "He will make your enemies, your foot stool."

Throughout the history of man, the table has been utilized to perform many tasks that help us in our day to day activities. *The Table of Content* is a list, usually found on a page before the start of a written work. *The Drafting Table* is a kind of multipurpose desk which can be used for any kind of drawing or impromptu sketching. And the *Billiard Table* is a table on which cue sports are played. For me, I like to eat. This cornucopia of bounty displayed on the cover is symbolic of the treasure in sonnet, rhythm and rhyme through poetry in **The Welcoming Table.** A banquet of the finer things that satisfy the soul.

Marrying these two concepts of peace and conspire, as I lavish my foe with goodwill is a recipe for internal strength and character. Metaphorically, the *"eating of my flesh as they stumble and fall",* adds to the narrative that the consumption of my benevolence brings detriment to the soul.

Keeping the motif of eating and "preparing a table" for my guest, I write a modest section of recipes in my book. I'd remembered the one thing my mother would say about all of her children, "they will never go hungry." Momma taught me how to cook. It is here I'd like to share just some of the Thornton's cuisine which again is symbolic of *"preparing a table."*

The essays are parts of my life that's riddled with humor, memories and self-reflection. It's a section that lend itself to research as I delve into the Gullah people of South Carolina and our Historical Black College and Universities (HBCU). And an opportunity for me to say thank you in the essay, *"You Gave Me A Song."*

Once again I'd like to thank many who influenced me in this project. I thank the creator for using me in ways I thought impossible. To the reader. I sincerely hope *The Welcoming Table* does for you what it did for me. Lift the soul. Enjoy.

Thank You

to those who helped me through the difficult times

Sarah Churchill,
Maurice (Moe) Taylor
Jacqueline Thomas and
Lacricia Core

Thank you grandma for the gift of education.
Elizabeth (Susie) Booth-Thornton
1906 -2002

Content

Recipes and Essays

More Poetry-Continued

The Welcoming Table

Psalm 23:5

Thou preparest a table before me, in the
presence of mine enemies.

Those who encroach upon my territory.
Who conspire, to seek me out.

Who's intrigue; making secret plans –
doing something illicit – at my own
detriment; they've plotted about.

Come, set down at my expense and feast.
For those of you coming from the North,
South, West and East.

Bring all of your acrimony
       your heresy
       your dissent
       and folly at my demise.

"Then trod me in the very dirt,
But still like dust I'll rise." [1]

This bitter ,

    hostile

        rancor

            caustic

                complicity

That's the fuel I need to propel
me into a state of nobility.

Welcome.

---

1. Maya Angelou; Still I Rise

John Lewis
Good Trouble
1940 – 2020

Not even a quarter of a century old I stood amongst
a King to deliver my speech on the March on Washington.

I followed this monarchy with every fiber of my being.
SNCC was the motivating vehicle to align my aim to a
more peaceful protest.

I use my body as a symbol for civil rights. It was Bloody
Sunday that became my claim to fame; as I took one across
the head in the rights for freedoms name.

"We want our freedom; and we want it NOW! was the
cry I use to say. It's the same cry – "Black Lives Matter"
is the cry they want to convey.

On Pettus Bridge I shed the blood our freedom we
know is truest. Just give it time, renaming of the bridge
will be John R. Lewis.

3

From Selma to Montgomery their purpose was
the vote. They signed their Last Will in Testament
collectively they all have wrote.

Been eighty years – being seen in congress
as we sat in the chambers below. For gun laws
to be passed today; while the blood continues
to flow.

In America streets; and America's schools; and
America where we pray. Our Second Amendment
Rights - with bodies is how we pay?

"Good Trouble" is the thing you want; getting
clubbed, jailed and arrest. Good Trouble is
the plan sought after in lawful, peaceful protest.

Poetry

*Poetry, is something you write in the old
fashion way. Free style, using cursive or
print as a way to express yourself in
intangible terms.*

*Good poetry comes from learned experiences
tried and true;
Of moments God allows us to be tested,
and the things we go through.*

*Like in chemistry, covalently – poetry is a
shared entity.
It's the sharing of what's true about how
the world really is – as a form of entertainment,
therefore, feeding the soul.*

*Poetry has become my pulpit, my church
my cross.
Poetry is about everything gained; and the
truth about all that I lost.*

*Poetry is that gift to maneuver word and
speech into a language, only the in-tuned
ear can hear.*

*Poetry is that language that the author holds
so sacred, so dear.*

*Of course, if you don't get it – you don't
get it.*

MOREHOUSE

In 1867 of Augusta's basement home.
The home of Springfield Baptist where
the legacy of men are grown.

Coulter, Turney and White were the
pioneers of this dream; to educate young
boys to men was the purpose of this theme.

Its beginning was the Institute having 40
students enrolled. Dr. Roberts was its first
president as historian of old have told.

The institute offered studies that these
black men often seek. In Algebra, Geometry,
Latin, Philosophy and The New Testament
in Greek.

By 1879 the school had become a visionary.
It moved up north now it's called the
Atlanta Seminary.

The Baptist faith generated this collegiate entity; of sweat; and blood; and tears; and toil which gave it, it's dignity.

In 1913 and thousands of dollars more, it's my honor to announce. This grand institution of the South, we call it dear Morehouse.

Musically, the college has seen 100 plus some years. From Kemper Harrell; and Wendell P.; we lift our glass and cheer.

The millennial God grace the one to lead us for tomorrow. With precision, structure and the discipline as in Dr. David Morrow.

As we sing our mantra; of college days, "Brothers in Song, Sing On." The passing years that bind us dear and the friendships that are so strong.

"Dear old Morehouse, dear old Morehouse,
We have pledged our lives to thee;
And we'll ever, yea forever
Give ourselves in loyalty.

True forever, true forever,
To old Morehouse may we be;
So to bind each son the other
Into ties more brotherly.

Holy Spirit, Holy Spirit,
Make us steadfast, honest, true,
To old Morehouse, and her ideals,
And in all things that we do." [1]

---

1.   J. O. B. Moseley, "Dear Old Morehouse"

Scabs, When Left Alone

To pick a scab, of crusted blood,

in use for protecting a wound.

Of incident, accident or trauma –

will heal, not later but soon.

A scab is thought as repairmen,

involvement of several things.

Fibronectin is first,

      it releases protein

         and healing is what it brings.

Fibrinogen, covert to Fibrin

      And Fibrin acts as a mesh.

Which triggers the enzyme

      of Thrombin and such,

where clotting performed at its best.

In nature, the way to heal –

Is enacted, as mentioned above.

But the spirit has a way

to heal void of science

    to heal is an act of love.

        To scar is a reminder, of such

Of something or someone went wrong.

The sharing with others

    in time of pain

Not weak, but that you're made to be strong.

So when things get damaged, sometimes they

do, things you don't condone.

Just remember the rule – scabs are best,

are best when left alone.

Rhetorical Dance

*When you say something, tried, intended to make
a point. An unusual phrase; with thought, to
spare the hearer of disappoint.*

*When you form your words to shield your subject
of embarrassment in advance. It's when your
tone begins to do; to do the rhetorical dance.*

*When you substitute your choice of words that
may seem to harsh or blunt. And thinking later,
with whom you speak, you really don't want
to confront.*

*The person in question, and what you say in
informal rants and chants. The unpleasant
way to ward off exposure is in the rhetorical
dance*

12

Lincoln's Soliloquy

Emancipation Proclamation

January 1, 1862

President Lincoln is in his office. He paces the room in thought about the state of affairs of this nation. He takes a seat behind his desk as he gazes out of his window as his conscience begins to speak aloud.

My ultimate objective in this struggle is

to save the Union. Whether slavery

persist or abate, it will be as an indirect

result of my efforts to restore the commonwealth

and stability this country so desperately

needs. What I do about slavery and the

colored race, I do only as to utilize that energy

source at every cause possible in reclaiming

the object of my desire; this country.

We who breathe the air of the North feel in

some way that slavery is morally wrong.

But my heart does not give way to sympathy-

Nor am I in accordance with the bleeding-

heart Abolitionist to free the slaves on compassion

alone. There are much greater concerns. Salvaging America.

I do not own any slaves, nor do I care to.
But I have been known to support Union
Commanders who have returned run-a-way
slaves to their rebel masters. Again my attitude,
concerns and feelings about the institution of
slavery goes undisturbed. However, I am
shaken when I see this Union on the verge of
destruction and disharmony because of slavery.

Lock-Step Wizard

In lock-step they march off to lost
    To the voice and the tune, they call boss.
        With one accord; they're comfortably aboard
            No matter of the mind-set or cost.

        They all pledge allegiance to the man.
      The one with small hands and orange tan.
   His second time around; with foreign help that was found,
A repeat of a debacle once again.

Russia are you listening to the cries.
    Of the one who pathologically lies.
        With envy of the man; before him he would despise
           Of being awarded the piece Nobel Prize.

        Impeachment, trashing opponents with Ukraine.
     For November Elections so that he could remain.
   The liar in chief, xenophobic and cheat
putting our country in a lot of suffrage and strain.

The guardsmen with their loyalty to him.

As if he's like some princely diadem.

Singing praises unto him, like in churches holy hymn.

He lacks the shine and gloss of a gem.

You know it's all about the Mr. "Who"

With his narcissistic and outlandish point of view.

When everything goes right; just because his skin is white-

That narrative means it must be all so true.

And statements like, "they're good folks on both sides."

In Charlottesville on different political divides.

When race, the question is asked, his decision he just acts;

Like Wallace, Duke and Thurmond with great pride.

Now we're approaching all lock-step towards hell.

A most funky, pungent, scent, sniff of smell.

With COVID-19, a most horrendous scene –

All locked-down at the places that we dwell.

But according to our commander now in chief.

With his reckless, rash and selfish belief.

Puts lives in great danger, for an economy exchanger.

Our lives in the balance of eminent grief.

Whore Bath

When you hit-it and Quit-it. Or just sponge
it off. In a bowl, lil-soap, lil-water and a
dingy wash cloth.

In a hurry, now hit that neck and wash those
two armpits. Wash all around your belly button
and get right under those tits.

Clean up that hiid, wash around your waist
and don't forget your hips. Wash between
those cheeks and please don't forget those lips.

Make sure all the lipstick and the perfume
scent is gone. Let me get myself outta
here before the crack of dawn.

A car drove up -- "is that yo man", don't
want to feel his wrath. Imma get my things
together; the things for my whore bath.

17

Lunch Meat

Submarine Haven, Round O' Clock
Lil-Tavern and Micky D's.
Were the sandwich shops of
yester-year all that ate here were pleased.

Hardee's, Wendy's – Burger King
and Ann's, up the way –
were places that we'd go-n-eat
that made up our day.

Jimmy John's, Subway – Chipotle
are the newest on the scene;
of lunch meat shops, there're
all around, to eat and to convene.

What's novel of this growing trend,
are price-y seafood meals.
At Annapolis Seafood Market
is their lump; crab cake deal.

So, if you come down "Restaurant Row"

for assortment or a-kind.

Of various lunch meats,

old and new, are not hard to find.

This Dispensation Is Over

Just like the divine ordering
of the affairs of the world;
This *"Dispensation"* of those things
concerning the heart of my will
is over.

To abate, to expire,
the curtailing of –
To abort, to terminate;
the all around ceasing
to **give,** unapologetically
is over.

You can't expect me to be
the one who's going to pick
up the tab on this one –
not no more.

When incessantly asking me
for information – when in times

of my former self, there'd
be a burgeoning of rhetoric
out of my mouth – before I
would have the time to take
back what I had previously stated.

But I am much wiser now.

Programs, Programs and Programs!

Like the transit system of San Fran.
Just waiting on the next brainstorm
of a "program" – to jump on –
paying nothing, **"nada".**

With arms folded, settin' on hands,
bending to your will of doing **nada.**
Then smile and grin and say
 "that was fun, when we gonna
do that again"

Not hardly, because you see,
This Dispensation Is Over!

Ripping and running ….

and for what.

You'd be dead, gone and forgotten.

Then a still small voice says,

Aiight, bring it all in; before

you done gone on killing yourself.

Because this dispensation is over.

Little Foxes

We gather all life social ills
and compile them all as one.

We separate what's big – what's small
before the day is done.

We rationalize each sin, as though
we're God and His dear Son.

But even Christ, in all four gospels,
preached forgiveness for everyone.

It amazes me to think of you
in judgement that you keep.
On adultery, porn and lascivious
in each subject that you meet.

But to covet, glutton, lie and cheat
are those secret hidden sins –
are the "little foxes", I mentioned
before at start or begin.

Per chance that some don't make

it, upon Heaven's restful shore –

It's the "little fox" that has kept you

lost; outside eternals door.

Enmity

Some things are virtually baked in

Decades of being vexed at something
that's bigger than you and I.

At my demise, my misfortune
gave you hope that it all was
coming to an end.

But circumstances made things
clearer for me – unfortunately.

Of all the presumed folly and misdeeds –
you've manage to escape. DAMN-IT!

Cuz, in spite of those clandestine
heart-filled hopes -- you'd survived
it all.

Out of the darkness of life attacks
what I saw of you, no chance of coming back.

But that damn shift in the atmosphere –

made it all clear.

The act of God's love of labor,

He's kept me in His favor

and His cosmos; a well-ordered stratosphere.

I'm sure you couldn't have

known this –

that my relationship insist;

That with God the Father –

and Christ the Son,

that discernment is in order to exist.

Maryland, My Maryland

Annapolis to the Eastern Shore

Maryland, My Maryland

Patuxent to Old Baltimore

Maryland, My Maryland

The counties all of twenty-four

Mc Henry's Fort we won the war

Lush foliage green on forest floor

Maryland, My Maryland

The path of Harriet Tubman's way

Maryland, My Maryland

Route freedom through Chesapeake Bay

Maryland, My Maryland

The poet Poe is on display

Of Raven's bird, the bird of prey

God bless this state with move and sway

Maryland, My Maryland

In medicine we chart the course
Maryland, My Maryland
Johns Hopkins is the place of choice
Maryland, My Maryland

At Sharpesburg of Antietam Fort
The Union Army fought with force
That battlefield our hearts remorse
Maryland, My Maryland

Our treasured fowl, the oriole
Maryland, My Maryland
From Chevy Chase to Camp Parole
Maryland, My Maryland

Allegiance to our flag we hold
Hands on our hearts – salute the pole
Like "Crab Cakes" on a Kaiser Roll
Maryland, My Maryland

As president and senate make
Maryland, My Maryland
The Academy is where they rate
Maryland, My Maryland

Jimmy Carter make no mistake
And John McCain his to partake
Is where they spent four years it take
Maryland, My Maryland

Now that we pledge our lives to thee
Maryland, My Maryland
That all men are created free
Maryland, My Maryland

Regardless of my pedigree
Death by your own white oak tree
So let this day you shall decree
Maryland, My Maryland

Written June 25th, 2020

Bruce D. Thornton

----------*----------

I Do Not Approve

First of all, a whole rack of folks
you'd be disqualifying.

Just in the life of those who wake
up with this albatross hanging around
your neck; we manage.

And to borrow one moment of our
lives, is a cautionary note that you
have the luxury of never having
to know.

To peep and hide, having no sense
of pride – you go on with the thought,
not to care.

To duck and dodge with the hope
of a mirage – our lives a constant
scare.

I Do Not Approve!!!!
It's lazy of you to say.
No thought or concern,
of how they became that way.
And who among you campaigned
for the shame of a lifetime to be
called a sissy, queer, punk, a fag
----- a expletive (M F); tea bag.

A dyke, queen and butch
a lover of gays; undoubtedly
------ a expletive (G D); fag hag.

You know, it takes a whole lotta
courage waking up to face the
day to day. That's courage baby.
The courage you can't even say.

And Miss, I Do Not Approve! – (snap)
You don't know good courage, like
I know good courage. [1]

So be grateful of the love
that was intended to reproduce.

Instead of the activity; at an age,

where instinctively you've been introduced.

---

1 Sommore; The Queens of Comedy, 2000

Hooves

He's not wearing any shoes today!
No Florsheims, or Gucci
Ferragamo or Lucchesi.

No Adidas, no Jordans
or New Balance, no Nike.

Nah; the shoes he wears
are made from the horny cells
made within.

Liken to an extension of the
nailbed of keratin.

Fashioned as though he's been
walking on stilts –
Hovering over the administration
that he built.

On Russia's collusion

and the nineteen others are

thought as confusion?

No sir – you said, "You could

grab them by the pussy."

Now that's what you said!!!!

Cuz all you got to do is be famous.

Isn't there a smell that's is congruent

with wearing those pumps, Mr. T_ _ _ _?

In suit and tie –

he's dressed from head to ….

But the toe is an unusual appearance.

Beastly at best; or the mark of.

In Greek Mythology; like centaur

except standing on two legs.

HOOVES; (hallelujah) – that stands on the promises of God.

Blocking the way of sinners, who not

knowing is therefore, following a fraud.
HOOVES; (Jesus) – that trample over the
party, who put him there.
Now keeping the "R" party hostage
and therefore, left for scared.

Like a cancer, growing on America's ass.
and its oncologist named Mueller –
from his own party, has to perform
a certain task.

And the firing of Preet ---- Obstruction
              Comey – Obstruction
              Yates --- Obstruction
              Flynn --- Obstruction
              Sessions --- Obstruction
and the resignation off Reince, Priebus,
and Sean Spicer.

Can't you see him walking across the White
House lawn.
Trampin', Trampin' – Tryin' to make H_ _ _
my home, Hallelujah, I'm trampin' – trampin'
I'm tryin' to make H_ _ _ my home.

Give me the dirt on Biden – B
Cause if you don't then Ten Billion
Dollars you ain't gonna see.

An impeachable offense
The Dems couldn't get me
That's past-tense.

I'm on some new stuff; the Dems tryna
put on us. Now here come hoax of the
coronavirus.

Now I won't give its true name;
the true name that it's due.
I'll called it one of my racist names'
I'll call it the Kung flu.

Unbridled Emotion

Let me see you laugh and not ashamed
to show your teeth.

Let me see you sing – mouth open wide,
Unknown to others the sound that you bring.

When you cry; let me see your tears
while the world is attentive.

In Anger – Straight Out, that emotion
when you become argumentative.

When a person shows you who they are,
it is up to you to believe.
In jealousy; the heart of the matter, it's
theirs to conceive.

Lord, Bless Me on This Street

Lord, bless me on this street
And for all the neighbors that I meet.

To give us comfort for this day,
On watch and keep, I daily pray.

And for those we've lost a while ago –
Nelson, Humphies the Scotts – a blow.
To Peters, Long and Cassy Hoe –
and the Thorntons, all lived on Marengo.

Ten, Thirty and Fifty He keeps,
Are miles to go before I sleep
Of stroke of kidney you've been Thee aid
I've overcome the struggles of life had made.

And when the time; my maker I meet
Lord bless all who dwell upon this street.

Don't Handle Me

For years I wondered if I could get by.

Shameful of the chores of sibling try.

Now a man with certain qualities.

> *Don't handle me!*

Family gatherings my duty was to make cake.

Chocolate, Pound, Bundt was mine to create.

Displeased of how the task caused belittling.

> *Don't handle me!*

My sis, would make her list at Mr. Corn's Store.

Of Reese's Cup and Barbeque Corn Chips; a treat
she'd often adored.

At fifteen, my burdened soul found liberty.

> *Don't handle me!*

"Mercy there was great-and grace was free.

Pardon there was multiplied to me –

There my burdened soul found liberty." [1]

> *Don't handle me!*

---

1. William R. Newell, 1895   Moody Bible College

Mathematics

(Dedicated to Brandon Rowe)

"Broadneck High School"

Narrative:

I am employed at the Anne Arundel County Board of Education as a substitute teacher. My school of choice is Broadneck High School. I'm most often seen in the Math Department there. I had a conversation with a teacher about my extra-curricular activities and it was at this time he understood my love of poetry; conversely, my never understanding of the concepts of mathematics. You see, algebraically – the letters are meant for English classes; leave the numbers for Math. He said to me why not write a poem about Mathematics. I replied, "nah man, that's a hard nut to crack." He said to me, "Bruce that would be a perfect way to expound on your aversion to this subject matter. So I picked up pencil and put it to paper and I came up with these words. Not an aversion – just some mathematical concepts. This is for you, Brandon Rowe.

In Geometry, there are cylinders.

There're rectangle – triangles to use.

The length of a right-sided angle;

is called a hypotenuse.

In calculus – a higher form of math

where man's thought processes is capital.

In calculus and the violin; the shape

and the symbol is integral.

40

Pi = 3.14159265359 …

On March 14th; we celebrate

that Pi as apple, blueberry

and key lime.

If These Grounds Would Speak

The Freedman Bureau managed Southern lands
that had been abandoned during this civil war…yet furthermore

Over one million acres of this war-torn property
was parceled, leased or rented out to former slaves…that braved

Though barren and desolate; the impoverishment
of this homeland became the hope for millions of
African-American ancestors who had toiled, bled
and died for this moment in history…capturing the victory

The forsaken land of battle and bloodshed became
the sacred ground upon which 117 historically
black institutions were found… profound

On these hallowed grounds stand monuments of
our people. A landmark of history, in the struggles
of a people who with their lives paid for the
opportunity of you being here. In order that you
might have a better life, through an enriched education… of a nation

Oh, if these grounds would speak.

The Keeper of This House

I am the keeper of this House
The bills; the up keep, I do without a spouse.

I am liken unto Joshua,
"but as for me and my house"
there is this thing; I will announce.

You can't run up in here, disrespecting
the ebb and flow – because of what you
think, and what you don't even know.

Coming by my house when you know
I'm not there.
To seek folly and disruption,
no conscience, no care.

This is my house
      Willed to me by my father;
      the JET

43

No mistake; both God and I are not
through with it yet.

Repairs are done consequently.
When I have the money, I'll
construct where the need may be.

The house I knew, in its glorious past.
Having family and friends; making
the memories to last.

Of the twenty-five years I have
kept his wishes –
All the money in the world,
couldn't replace how it enriches.

For I am the "Keeper of This House."

Songs in the Key of Life

If I Were a Carpenter
They'd be no reason for me to be
a Rolling Stone. Because after all
the rolling stone would only:
Run ...Run ...Run ...

But, Love is Here and Now You're Gone.
And I keep asking myself – Baby, Baby
Where Did Our Love Go?

But you still keep on moving; with
No Where to Run; and No Where to Hide.
So, you'd end up Back in my Arms Again.
Cause true love is Like an Itching in my
Heart.

That's why, Baby I Need Your Loving.
I'm only asking you to be My Girl.
I know it sounds like I'm pleading
But, I Ain't too Proud to Beg.

Love is a powerful potion; a remedy
known only by a physician, but My
Baby Must be a Magician, Cause She
Sure has the Magic Touch.

Now when left alone, it would make
sense to Ask the Lonely. Simply because
the life they're living is measured by
no one around; like the Tears of a Clown.

Like a Ball of Confusion spun out of
control, with the possibility of taking
a Shotgun to the head all because
What Becomes of a Brokenhearted;
Who's just having a Love Hangover
Not wanting a cure for this …
Don't call the doctor; nor the preacher.

Now Burnette, Heard it Through the
Grapevine, by calling Beechwood 4-5789
That's how she found out What's Going On.

All this tragedy, caused by love has gotten
A Stubborn Kind of Fellow Whose got his
Mind Made up to Love You.
So when moments of disconcertion between
a lover, companion, your wife. Remember
these elements, these songs; the Songs in the
Key of Life.

COVID-19

The Coronavirus

This foreign agent of pan appeal has gotten its
victims as the reports reveal.

Respiratory in nature: cough, sneeze, spit or snot
Is this virus of change that the world has got.

The severity between the flu and COVID-19
Is the immunity of new, that this pandemic means.

Corona time on surface, nobody seems to know.
From a few hours to several days, the life of this
virus can grow.

What happens if you get this bug, what symptoms
to expect. There's fever, cough, aches and pains
with COVID to suspect.

If contracted COVID-19, and with pets is my concern.
No licking of face, no petting; take caution that you've
learned.

The virus started in China; hit Italy and Spain
the most. It even reached the USA doing
damage from coast to coast.

The rule is stand six feet apart, wear
gloves and wear a mask. The distance we put
between us, is a required daily task.

So COVID or Corona, whatever you choose
to say. This silent killer, this agent of loss is
upon us here today.

This Thing Wasn't Done in a Corner

-------------------- ACTS 26:26 --------------------

Bishop Wilbert L. Baltimore

Paul spoke freely to King Agrippa and to Festus,

…" that I once was Saul who persecuted those who

believed in Jesus for all …."

"I liken myself to him… the things not hidden

from them."

This Thing Wasn't Done in a Corner

Out in my prime. Nebulous to those things regarding

my spiritual growth and well-being. But moments of

clarity pierced my cortex reminding me to stay woke

for fear of my going astray.

I was OUT… with Jesus on my lips; and a praise

in my heart. Straddling the two worlds miles apart.

Rolling around in Gods mouth like lukewarm

watermelon on a hot July day. On the cusp of

being spewed because inability to obey.

50

But God uses whom He chooses to be that
effective witness. Like salt in collard greens;
giving seasonings and taste while I run this race.
Blessed quietness ordinarily don't save souls.

So my appreciation of this relationship is
noteworthy to me …The grace and mercy
that was extended at Calvary. The lest thy
forget Gethsemane, and lest thy forget thy agony.

So I cry out YES; to "Won't He Do It."
And shout YES; to "I said I wasn't gonna tell
nobody – I Couldn't Keep It To Myself."
Oh, but "He that hath a ear, let him hear"…1
that …… *This Thing Wasn't Done in a Corner*

"I said I wasn't Gonna Tell Nobody"

"I said I wasn't gonna tell nobody"

And I was right!

Had to keep this for myself

Nothing personal

It's just as I live and breathe –

as I get older

I'm done making stupid mistakes;

made in the past.

 "I said I wasn't gonna tell nobody"

I TELL YOU EVERYTHING

And as quiet as it's kept –

What I say.

You use it against me.

Oh, you don't mean me no harm

You just got the case of the logorrhea

You can't hold water from there to here-a

Telling you is like telling folks

from Detroit to Bengazi.
You done gone on to tell
Lotti – Dotti and errybody.

Your circle of friends; are my friends too.
Our circle of friends will pursue her, him
and you.

It's like folks calling you out of your name.
In answering them – you've only answered
their claimed.

Conversely, the vile things you hear
them say;
Don't respond to it – they will eventually
go away.

When reputations seem to be
going south.
My only quest is to keep my
name outta your mouth.

These Are They

Revelation 7: 14

These are they who have come out of great tribulation.

Who straighten their back and claimed this revelation.

These are they who have marched their last time for hope.

To be respected and counted as a people having the vote.

These are they who have washed their robes for peace.

In the name of Jim Crow, the Poll Tax, so that new day

Lynching would cease.

These are they …..

Recipes and Essays

Aunt Bertha's Biscuits

¼ cup of warm water

1 ½ teaspoons of active dry yeast {1/2 of a package }

1 teaspoon of granulated sugar

2 ½ cups Bisquick baking mix

½ teaspoon of baking soda

1 Tablespoon of butter {soften }

½ cup of buttermilk

Directions:

Butter 9-inch cake pan. Coat it with flour. Set aside.

In a small bowl, add the yeast and sugar to the warm water. In a warm, draft free area for five (5) mins.

In a large bowl, add the baking mix [Bisquick], baking soda, butter, buttermilk and the yeast mixture until well blended.

Lightly dust with additional baking mix and knead the dough about 10 to 12 times until smooth. Cut out 7 to 8 biscuits.

Place biscuits into prepared pan ……. cover with a clean towel, in a warm; draft free area for 30 minutes... biscuits should rise. Place biscuits in buttered and flour coated pan.

Bake at 400 degrees for 10 minutes.

The Washboard

My earliest recollection of the washboard was when I lived on Charles Street in the mid to late sixties. I remember it sitting in the corner, nestled between the stove and the hot water heater. My mother would go in the kitchen and pull it out ever so often when the washing machine just couldn't get out that stain from my father's barbering jacket. I'd watch her tirelessly scrub and scrub with the use of Borax laundry detergent while beads of sweat formed around her brow.

The washboard to me, just an old metal cleaning apparatus, rectangular in shape, with a series of ridges or corrugations centered in a wooden frame for which to scrub clothes clean. My shirt, my brother drawers and my sister panties have all seen the likes of the washboard from time to time.

My mother had a routine for washing clothes. She'd fill up the machine with soapy water and when the cycle began for washing, the machine had a certain sound or rhythm in the process of cleaning clothes. It was music. The repetitive cadence (if you dared to pay attention), would make one bend and sway to its own rhyme. Think about it. The washing machine could have been your first introduction of keeping time. Unconsciously, this repetition is a friend to dance. In our cognitive minds the mechanics of how the nuts and bolts of making this engine functioned coupled with the sloshing around of wet garments: shirts to sheets, pant to panties and jeans to a jersey made that sound which was music to the ear.

But the washboard had one initial function in a bucket of soapy water and the pressure of hands to scrub clothes clean. However, out of the bucket and into the hands of a Pentecostal worshipper the washboard took on a more musical connotation.

It had been nearly twenty years before I'd discovered this duality in an apparatus to clean clothes and a percussion instrument for making music. With a washboard and a spoon, feet that would stomp and clapping hands would give the propensity of a church to break out in a shout. I'm talking about what a washboard could do. I'm quite aware of how the church has progressed in the way of instrumentation. But this segment is about where the Black Church came out from a Pentecostal perspective. It's not about the piano synthesizer, having the capability of horns, violins and the sounding of drums. No. I'm talking about a time when you used what you had and the glory of the Lord was fulfilled in a place. I'm talking about a place in history where the rudiments of worship sustained a people with the hope of a better day. The washboard is a symbol of how meager means can generate a certain quality of praise. A praise unfettered by the accouterments that we have today.

Now in all seriousness, I wouldn't suggest we all put down the Grand Piano, do away with the Hammond Organ or scale back the use through mediation the technology that's been afforded in this climate of praise and worship. My only means is for us to embrace those things in our collective and familiar past. To hold dear in the archive of remembrance our humble beginnings. Then we as a people can appreciate Gods use of mankind knowledge that has propelled us into a higher understanding and level for which to *praise God in His sanctuary.*

"Praise ye the Lord. Praise God in his sanctuary;
praise him in the firmament of his power.
Praise him for his mighty acts: praise him according
to his excellent greatness.
Praise him with the sound of the trumpet: praise
him with the psaltery and harp.
Praise him with the timbrel and dance: praise him
with stringed instruments and organs." [1]

---

1. Bible; Psalm 150: 1-4, KJV

Bruce's Macaroni and Cheese

1 block of Velveeta

1 block of mild cheddar cheese

1 bag of shredded cheddar, mozzarella and Colby

1 box of ziti, penne or shells pasta

2 teaspoons of salt

2 teaspoons of pepper

1 stick of butter

¼ cup of milk

2 cups of water – (boiling of your choice of pasta)

1 *In boiling water, place 1 box of pasta in the water, adding 1 cap of vegetable oil.*
2 *Boil for 20 minutes*
3 *After 20 minutes, drain pasta into a cullender/colander bowl*
4 *Place pasta in baking dish.*
5 *Mix in your salt and pepper*
6 *Combine ¼ cups of milk and sliced velveeta cheeses into a separate saucepan and slowly melt. Note: start this at the same time that you boil the pasta.*
7 *When velveeta melts ……. Pour it onto the pasta*
8 *Grade 1 block of your mild cheddar (in grader: large) or cube it by hand.*
9 *Chop butter into 8 slices and strategically place them evenly with pasta*
10 *Preheat oven, bake at 325 degree for 25 minutes.*
11 *When done …… immediately spread your bag of 3 cheeses: cheddar, mozzarella and Colby onto pipping hot macaroni and cheese*
   ---------------------------- serves 8 --------------------------------

59

Relax in There

Leslie, Ronnie and Bruce. It was time for our yearly physical and Momma was the LPN in this family. We were all so squeamish around this time and not looking for, what we thought a grueling experience. Every orifice was poked and prodded every-which-way. Now that I am older, I understand what my mother was searching for. Now I understand why.

I have a buddy, Lionel, we would often recite various portions of the movie, "The Color Purple." Our favorite passage in the movie was ... *"for you can say, Amen."* I'll let you think about that for a minute.

Living on Charles Street in the sixties, this examination had the feel of a surprised bed check like they would do in prison, in search of foreign contraband. We never knew when Momma was scheduling our exam.

I and my other siblings were three years apart. Leslie was the oldest, then Ronnie, then me. One thing my mother never changed, the order of the examination. She'd start with the oldest to the youngest. All three of us had to endure the thermometer in the anus routine. Leslie and Ronnie seemed to be okay, but I was a different matter. I remembered that experience and how tensed I was even before the point of contact. I imagine, upon entry, that my sphincter muscles gripped the thermometer with force. My mother tried to get me to take it easy while she continued her examination. Between the rumbling of the exam and my outward burst of displeasure, I would hear my father in his bedroom shouting, "Relax, Relax, Relax in There."

60

It's been fifty-seven years since I heard those words. Remembering seems to make me laugh. What made this experience so different from my other siblings? What was I doing that caused my father to react in that manner? One has to wonder. *"Relax in There"* has a number of connotations for me to ponder. Could it be just the response of hearing a seven year old boy uncomfortable with this particular procedure? After all, my brother was only three years my senior, and he didn't behave in this manner. Or could it be something far more cognitive; something more telling about this Bruce? Maybe my dad knew of me before I knew myself. Could this have been a *trigger* of something as parents we often don't like to talk about? Was this a cry that was muted for the fear of having to accept a lifetime of embarrassing moments. Moments that would occur in the most inopportune of times.

I'm often reminded of a particular scripture in St. John 9:1-3, when the disciples asked Jesus, *"who sinned, this man or his parents, that he was born blind."* And Jesus answered, *"Neither this man nor his parents sinned, but that the works of God should be revealed in him."* I'm not claiming to be a **wonder,** as the folks of the Pentecostal sect would have it. But God has this. A friend once said to me, "you know God don't make no mistakes," and my response was "I know, because he made me." Now that may seem blasphemous to a few, but I believe we in our finite minds collectively breathe the air that is anoxic into our social mores. We impose what we don't understand to the broad swath of humanity as ideals. Now this topic of homosexuality has its place in the broader since to be discussed, but let's have this discussion from a *nature* or *nurture* point of view. The age of consent does not apply to the heterosexual or homosexual when born in the mind at an early age. It's either one or the other. Right or wrong, that's the way it is. I write in the poem, *I Do Not Approve, "So be grateful of the love you have, intended to reproduce. Instead of the activity at a young age, instinctively you've been introduced."* So before you brow beat, ostracize and cast condemnation on something you haven't given your full attention, consider that God has made us all different. He has given to some, shoulders broader than others. Then the question is as to why? And the answer come to mind, *"My grace is sufficient."*

As for me, it's been both a humbling yet a vigilantly chartered course. I've been in places and situations only a God could deliver me from. I've had people come and go in my lifetime. Doing some of the same things, yet I am still here. Why? Because I'm honest with God and I found out the key to my success, that's having a relationship with Him. I'm sixty-four right now. And just shy of being sixty-five, I've come into my own; knowing my own voice and a self-aware man in this new millennium. William Shakespeare writes in the play of Hamlet, where *Polonius* tells of *Laertes,* "This above all-to thine own self be true."

Rice with Sweet Peas and Broccoli Florets Casserole

2 ½ cups of rice

2 cups of chicken broth

1 cups of water

1 can of condensed cream of chicken soup

2 teaspoon of salt

1 ¼ teaspoon of pepper

3 pinches of parsley flakes

1 can of small early peas

1 ½ of crown broccoli

add broccoli just as the rice beginning to turn white estimate of 25 mins.

A mixture of 3 to 4 cheeses .... Do the same with the cheese.

In a Dutch Oven Skillet – bake at 325 degree, for 45 minutes

As soon as it comes out of the oven .... Top with mild cheddar, parmesan and Colby Jack cheeses

Serve 15 minutes out of the oven. Fry yourself some chicken, and you got a meal goin' on.

Lessons Learned

This segment of The Welcoming Table is to pay homage and highlight some of the Historically Black Colleges and University, whereby I give a brief synopsis of the history of that institution.

Hampton University

It would speak of Hampton University which was founded in 1868, under the Union Army Brevet General Samuel Chapman Armstrong on a 120 acre farm. Known at the time as Hampton Normal and Agricultural Institute, it opened its doors having only 2 teachers and 15 students. Hampton's purpose was to educate those who were called to teach our youth and become the pioneers in educating those who lived in rural communities. During the late 1800's the University began programs which not only served to educate blacks and the Native American. This program was called the Indian Educational Program and lasted 4 decades. In 1871, fifteen men and five women made up the institutions first graduating class and four years later Hampton's most illustrious alumnus Booker T. Washington graduated in 1875. [1]

---

1.   Special Collection Library/Hampton University

Grambling State University

From the Allen Green Store. To North Louisiana Agriculture and Industrial School. To Louisiana Negro Normal and Industrial Institute, to its present name. **If these grounds would speak**, it would speak Grambling State University.

Under the leadership of Lafayette Richmond, the school began in 1869 when the farmers of North Louisiana had hopes of educating their youth. On 23 acres of land, owned by a black man (John Monk), it was purchased at $5.00 an acre. Close to the turn of the century, members of the Color Agricultural Relief Association asked Booker T. Washington of Tuskegee Institute for assistance in the proper operation of an industrial school. He in response sent his protégé Charles P. Adam to pave the way for the institution.

On November 1, 1901 the newly organized school opened with 3 teachers and 125 students. The boarding and tuition fee at the time was $5.00 per month. Those who couldn't afford to pay; paid in commodities such as peas, potatoes, yams etc. During Grambling's formative years its course of studies were: Methods to improve farming; preparation and preserving foods; improving health and sanitary conditions; how to buy property and the building of homes. In addition, learning the 3R's. [2]

---

2. Special Collection/Grambling State University

Talladega College

If this ground would speak, it would speak about the convention held at Mobile, Alabama where 56 black men were the start of an idea which lead to the academic success of thousands of Black Americans nationwide. On November 20, 1865 William Savery and Thomas Tarrant (former slaves from Talladega) left this meeting excited about educating their youth. Their excitement had stimulated their rural community to the point that they all agreed to start a school.

In its beginning, the dream was born in a 2-room house over crowded by students who were thirsty for knowledge. The Educational Society learned of this and bought an old carpet shop where meager renovations were made. This served as Talladega County's first black schoolhouse. Having received word that there was a 3-story brick building (built by ex-slaves on 34 acres of land; William Savery requested of General Wagner Swayne of the Freedmen's Bureau of Alabama) to assist him and the Talladegan community in the purchase of that $8000.00 property. It was at such time the General sought help from the American Missionary Society. The society's generosity became the result of another black institution, thousands of blacks educated, and an enlightened community. Thus, "Talladega College" was born. [3]

---

3.   Special Collection/Talladega College

Spelman College

If these grounds would speak, it would tell the story of Atlanta's own Spelman College. Formerly known as the Atlanta Baptist Female Seminary. This school began when two women of New England were commissioned by the Women's American Baptist Home Mission Society to open a school in the south to freed Negro women and girls. Sophia B. Packard and Harriet E. Giles received $100.00 from a fundraiser at the First Baptist Church of Medford, Massachusetts on March 6, 1881. On the 29th of the same month, they left for Atlanta in pursuit to educate black women. Arriving in Atlanta on April 1, they were advised by a Rev. D. Shaver, (a teacher at the Atlanta Baptist Seminary) who led them to Rev. Frank Quarles, the pastor of Friendship Baptist Church. On Monday, April 11, having 11 students, $100.00, a Bible, a pad and a pencil this school now known as Spelman College was opened in the basement of Atlanta's Friendship Baptist Church. [4]

4.   Special Collection/Spelman College

Howard University

These grounds would speak from the "Hilltop." The highest geographical landmark in the District of Columbia. Howard University began as a result of the First Congregational Society of Washington who ventured to establish a theological seminary for the training of black ministers. Before its present name, it was formerly known as the Howard Normal and Theological Institute for Educating Teachers and Preachers. A name in honor of Civil War hero and Commissioner of the Freedman Bureau, Major General Oliver Otis Howard. Howard University was founded on January 3, 1867 and it bears its present name.

Although, Howard is known as a black school, in May of 1867, four white girls (who were the daughters of the university trustees and faculty member) were the first occupants of this institution. Before the end of the first semester 90 additional students were enrolled. Within Howard's first 5 years of existence, it functioned as a University having 9 departments educating the youth of Washington, D.C. In 1873, financial support from the Freedman's Bureau was discontinued and the school functioned on private support. By 1928 the institution received its support from the government and Dr. Mordecai Wyatt Johnson, where he served as the school's first black president and administrator. Now this once 3-story red brick building (an earlier frame of this institution at the present site of the school's hospital) is known as the Mecca of black education. [5]

---

5. Special Collection/Howard University

F.A.M.U.

If this ground would speak, it would mention Florida Agriculture and Mechanical University. An institution which was founded on October 3, 1887 as the State Normal College for Colored Students. It began educating Black America with 2 teachers and 15 students. Within four years of its existence, its name changed to the State Normal and Industrial College for Colored Students. By 1909 the school had an enrollment of 317 students. Thomas DeSaille Tucker an attorney from Pensacola and Thomas Van Ronnasaler Gibbs, a state representative from Duvall County, were the pioneers of this great institution. However, under the administration of John Robert Edward Lee this school received most of its prominence and academic image it has today. [6]

---

6. Special Collection/Florida Agriculture and Mechanical University

Leslie's Herb Roasted Turkey

For 20 lb Turkey (serves 14)

Prepare by seasoning the turkey at least (6) hours before putting it in the oven.

<u>Turkey Rub</u>

2 teaspoons of salt
2 teaspoons of oregano
2 teaspoons of black pepper
1 tablespoon of sage
½ clove of garlic (crushed/blender)
2 sticks of butter (melted)
¼ cup of chicken/turkey broth (stock)
{refrigerate for 30 minutes}

Apply Rub: with gloves, rub down turkey with spices or without gloves, brush on turkey.

3 stalks of Rosemary: place one between each leg and wing; and the third stalk place in the cavity of the turkey.
2 stalks of celery, 1 large onion sliced in large quarters (4)

Bag It ………. Place turkey in refrigerator for 6 hours

Its Time to Roast: preheat oven at 325 degrees --- for (4)1/2 to 5 hours

Note: 1 hour after taking the turkey from oven, squeeze lemon over turkey. Remove all rosemary and onion from turkey.

You Gave Me a Song

We were preparing for the commencement of the graduating class of 1968, Annapolis Elementary School. It was a sunny morning in June. The exercises were held in the back of a red-brick three story building. Chairs were aligned for the seating of graduates and guest. The custodian had brought out an up-right piano for song. *Rev. Rufus Abernathy* was the music teacher at the time of my commencement. We had rehearsed for weeks and weeks the song entitled, "Halls of Ivy." It was the most beautiful melody and lyrics I had ever heard as an impressionable young man.

"In the hallowed halls of ivy

Where we live and learn to know –

That through the years we'll see you;

In the sweet after glow."

At the age of twelve, I received the Lord Jesus Christ as my savior. My Christian walk began at First Baptist Church on West Washington Street, Annapolis, Maryland. I was the youngest amongst the Thornton clan. My older siblings; Leslie and Ronald, respectfully, and I came to know our choir director Mr. Sammy Simms. Many were the friends I met at First Baptist: Oscar Kidd, Stanley Holland, Doris Belt, Valarie Williams, Denise and Kim Henderson, Karen Thomas, Thomasine Hawkins, Linda Postelweight, Clytie and Raynaud Simms and Claudia DeGrate, just to name a few. Together we were the young adult choir, but to us it was the "Sammy Simms" choir. I remember many songs but there was only one in particular that stayed with me through the years; "Walk on By Faith Each Day."

We cannot see in the future

And we cannot see through dark clouds

We cannot see through all of our tear drops

Walk on by faith each day; Walk on by faith

each day.

In 1974 I was nineteen, a high school graduate and had found a deeper understanding in my Christian walk. I came to know of a little Pentecostal church on the corner of Kirby Lane and Dorsey Avenue named, Holy Temple. I believe there was a call on my life that has shaped me to be the man I am today. The shepherd of this house was that of then, Rev. Baltimore; now Bishop Wilbert L. Baltimore. Musically endowed, he had the capacity to bring many of the young in the Annapolis area together in song in a way that was antithetical to the status quo. You see, Annapolis had only the choice of two faiths in which to worship. Baptist and the Methodist faith. Bishop Baltimore diversified religion within the framework of the black church and consequently the music as well. He brought Pentecostalism that these shores had not been accustomed and in theory not ready. Pentecostal, yet progressive, The Holy Temple Church Choir was on the church-wide circuit from coast to coast as an entity, recognized for its range in repertoire of music. From Anthems to Negro Spirituals to a more contemporary sound. From *Inflammatus* to *Ole Mary, Ole Martha* to *Climbing Up the Mountain,* this choir was versed to the extent they were prepared to perform at any venue with confidence. An original to Holy Temple was Bishop Baltimore's. *"If You're Happy."*

"If you're happy, and you know it

Say Amen – Say Amen.

If you're happy, and you know it

Say Amen – Amen.

If the spirit falls on you – make

you shout hallelujah.

If you're happy, and you know it

Say Amen – Amen"

Moreover, The Holy Temple family had a young man namely, Jeff Jacobs, now Dr. Jeff Jacobs. Jeff came to the Temple through the first migration of youth to have graced the doors of the little church on Kirby Lane and Dorsey Avenue. His humble beginnings came from a Methodist church on West Street – Asbury United Methodist Church. Asbury was a church steeped in tradition and known for its profound use of the anthem. Musically inclined, Jeff brought this genre of music to the Holy Temple archives. Such original as, *"Holy Is The Lord"* and *"Praise Ye The Lord."* However, Jeff's signature piece as a national recording artist of the song entitled, *"Delivered."*

It's through his blood, I've been delivered

Through his blood – I've been set free.

I've been washed in the blood of the lamb;

I've been set free, by God's own hand.

Delivered, Delivered, Delivered, Delivered

Delivered, Delivered, Delivered, Delivered

Delivered, Delivered; I've been set free.

In the early eighties, I left Annapolis for Atlanta as a student enrolled in the nations all male, predominantly black institution, Morehouse College. It was there I became a part of the world-renowned Morehouse College Glee Club under the direction of Dr. Wendell P. Whalum. The experience gleaned from this musical group exposed me to the classicals of Beethoven, Brahms and Schubert. I've gained a

75

greater appreciation of the knowledge of music having sung in Latin, Polish, German and African. But what impressed me the most was the simplicity of the old Negro Spirituals: *"I done done", Around de Glory Manger"* and *"On My Journey, Mount Zion."*

One day; One day- Mount Zion – I was walking along – Mount Zion

And the element sober – Mount Zion – and his love came down – Mount Zion

You can talk about me – Mount Zion – just as much as you please – Mount Zion

Imma talk about you – Mount Zion – When I'm on my knees – Mount Zion.

On my journey now – Mount Zion – On my journey now – Mount Zion

I wouldn't trade it for nothing – Mount Zion – On my journey now

Mount Zion.

In my sixty-four years of living I've found music to soothe the savage beast. In the moments that try men soul, music has been my comfort. *"A present help in the time of trouble"* [1]. When I was burdened you nurtured my life with a melody, bringing calm to the soul of my being. Without the warning of despair, you unknowingly saved a life, thought to be hurled out of control. Because of a song, peace was restored. *You gave me a song to sing; and I sang. Thank you.*

---

1. Psalm 46:1, The Bible, King James Version

Ollie's 7-Up Bundt Cake

3 cups of Gold Medal Flour
1 ½ sticks of butter (soften)
5 eggs (room temperature)
3 cups of sugar
2 Tablespoons of lemon extract
¾ cups of 7-Up (soda)

1st   cream sugar and butter
2nd   mix in your eggs -5 (one at a time)
3rd   mix in flour (1 cup stir, 2 cups stir, 3 cups stir)
4th   mix in 2 Tablespoons of lemon extract
5th   finally, fold in ¾ cups of 7-Up (soda)

Bake at 325 degrees
50 minutes to 1 hour   { test with tooth pick }
Let cool for 35 minutes …….. { flip upside down }

For Drizzle

3 cups of confectionary sugar
1 fresh lemon … {squeeze 3 Tablespoons into sugar }
3 Tablespoons of 7-Up
1 teaspoon of vanilla   {Mix all ingredients together }

When cake is fully cooled, drizzle glaze over cake.

*Garnish with lemon zest. And for presentation, try bordering the cake
with gardenia and its foliage or greenery of your choice.*

Enjoy

77

Gullah Music

In the early to mid-eighties, I attended a private all black male institution, namely Morehouse College. It was there that I sought out my love of music, as I found my way in the second tenor section of the Morehouse College Glee Club.

Under the direction of Dr. Wendell P. Whalum, we sang from a large repertoire of music. From Bach - All Breathing Life, to an original by Morrow, I Can't Tarry. From the South African – Nkosi Sikelel i Afrika, to Schubert-Die Nachtigall. From the English Christmas Carol-The Boar Head, to the Nigerian Carol-Betelehemu. But of all the songs we would sing, my favorite came from the heart and lips of the Gullah-Lawd, I Done Done.

The Negro Spirituals are really pure West African chants; brought over through the middle passage. It was the song of the slave and the reflection of their struggle. "I'm Building Me a Home", "Lawd, I Done Done" and "Pauline", were considered *Work Songs* of the slave. The Work Song became the fiber of black folk-lore music.

Its primary purpose was far from entertaining the masses or achieving capital gain; but served as a companion for over three hundred years to the sons and daughters coming from this *passage.* Singing these songs, dulled the pain of bodies having been beaten both by the sun and the whip. These songs, when sung, (despite the lash of the tongue), would excite the spirit which sustain the life of a people.

78

Songs that were sung during this time of our history, be it *work song* or otherwise, had duality in meaning. This meaning was quintessential of black folk freedom. Oh the harmony, humming and sway of blacken notes had its place in the hearts of those who sang it; but the symbolism of words was the sustenance that gave life to the song and to the people. In this two-fold expression, the slave would clandestinely sing songs that had the ability to communicate a stratagem amongst fellow slave-men. Yet at the same time, entertained the *master* with melodious tunes, leaving no trace or clue of abandonment to the plantation. Often the opinion of the plantation owner was that his slaves were carefree, mindless, adult children who hadn't a care in the world. They're singing, be it of jubilee or otherwise, was thought to be an intellectual deficiency. On the contrary, this race of people who had no education at all, relied on the strength of the song. Their intellectual deficiency was made up for with their ability to believe in a God who granted them this kind of wisdom to communicate. And, *"this people of song"*, had faith in one whom was predestined to lead her people out of the jaws of slavery; by way of escape. Harriet Tubman, the Moses of her people.

Bruce's Maryland Style Crab Cakes

The Mixture : 1 egg

¼ cup of Miracle Whip

2 Tablespoon of "French's" mustard

3 pinches of parsley flakes

2 pinches salt

2 pinches black pepper

2 pinches garlic salt

10 Premium Saltine Crackers (unsalted) crumbled, using rolling pin

2 Tablespoons of "Old Bay" seasoning

{ mix all ingredients together in bowl }

Crab Meat : { In a separate bowl }

2 tubs of "Special " Crab Meat   (pick out the remaining shells)

1 tub of "Lump" Crab Meat

Next, pour the contents of your mixture : Miracle Whip, salt, pepper into your "Crab Bowl".

With clean hands, fold the mixture into the crab, loosely.

Try not to break up the lump meat portion of the crab

Scoop up a ladle sized portion of crab meat; shaped into a ball

Set oven on Broil -- 300 degrees , for 20 – 25 minutes

Let cakes cool for 15 minutes. Squeeze (lightly) lemon juice over cakes

Serve with Premium Saltine Crackers, sliced tomato and your choice

cocktail sauce. Select your type of salad ... Garden Salad, Potato or Slaw.

With some iced tea …. Man, you ready to upset something …lol.

Oh … this should serve six (6)

Holding Up the Arms

Such were in the days of Moses, that John Lewis was assisted by a community who respected the right to a more peaceful protest on that bridge in Selma, when this community held up the arms of this living icon of civil rights. Sharpton, Abrams, Warren and Klobuchar were the witnesses to what was emblematic of a time far from the days of Aaron and Hur, when those men held up the arms of Moses. There is something that's born in the mind of Moses and John pivotal to their success about a movement. Seeing the work that they did was progress in motion but their absence of this continuum would be ongoing. It was the clarion cry of John to say, **"Don't Give Up, Don't Give In",** to the struggles that we would endure. For Psalm 30:5 says, "Weeping may endure for a night, but joy cometh in the morning".

Fifty-five years ago, seemingly, a peaceful day in March. To be exact, March 7, 1965 known as "Bloody Sunday". Gathered at the Brown Chapel AME Church were the marchers made up of "foot soldiers" – Hosea Williams, Jessie Jackson and Stokely Carmichael, and a whole host of people from the community who were hungry. Most importantly, the man who coined the term, **"Good Trouble"**, the iconic, John Lewis. The purpose of this assembly was for the right to the ballot box. Jim Crow laws in the south were so stringent that Black people of Selma, Alabama couldn't eat at the local McDonald during this time. They were voting for better jobs, better wages and for the dignity to be treated as decent human beings. There was a call for action, and as John would often say, **"We Want Our Freedom, and We Want It Now".**

On that day, they marched to the capitol which was in Montgomery. Approximately fifty miles away. Between Selma and

82

Montgomery lies the Alabama River and to cross it, you had to go over the Edmund Pettus Bridge. Leaving Brown Chapel they were lined up, two by two as they approach the bridge. They carried with them all that they owned. It's been reported that they all signed their "Last Will and Testament" the night before the march because there were no guarantees that they would make it with such harsh and brutal attacks.

Herein lies their struggle. This band of peaceful, non-violent protesters was faced with a blanket of police officers standing at the opposite side of the bridge. The greatest fear was leaving their survivors should anything happen to them. On the hearts and minds of those who marched was a brutal force whose interest was far from seeking the right to vote. Theirs was to vilify, destruct and dismantle every good and meaningful gesture to achieve equality and justice for all. Theirs was to trample over the civil liberties many had died for. Yet these marchers remembered Medgar Evers and Emmitt Till and countless others who lost their lives through such atrocities. They remembered the poll tax, the confederate flag and poor housing due to the districting of many states. Not being a juror because you don't have the right to vote. Gone are the days of the "curfew" and "show me your papers". Of being treated like chattel or being bought and sold as if we were property.

We have seen what fifty-five years of constant struggle looks like in America. And so we are here today, fifty-five years later commemorating that day on this bridge where John Lewis took one across the head for freedom sake. God allowed him to see eighty years of toiling for equality. He's gone now. So Sharpton is "holding up the arms" of him who can't do it for himself. Abrams is holding up his arms of voter suppression. Warren is holding up his arms for equal pay and universal health care. And Klobuchar holds up his arms for climate change for generations to come. The rest of us, as a community, we stand with this icon of civil rights knowing the words of his predecessor, Dr. Martin Luther King Jr saying, **"He's allowed me to go up the mountain, and I've looked, and I've seen the promise land. I may not get there with you. But I want you to know tonight, that we as a people will get to the promise land".** [1]

You know, when John spoke to the young people of today he would tell them that getting into trouble is alright. But make sure it's "Good Trouble". It's alright to get arrested sometime in peaceful protest. That's good trouble. Sometimes good trouble means that you might take one across the head for freedom sake. Good trouble. When you sit in the lower chamber with congress and refuse to move until the gun lobby does move, that's good trouble. I would often hold up my arms when officials charge me for disorderly conduct. I would hold up my arms in protest of "don't shoot". I would hold up my arms to cause no alarm. At eighty years old, now others would hold up my arms to do no harm.

---

1.   Dr. Martin Luther King Jr., Memphis, Tennessee; April 3rd, 1968

More Poetry

Word Salad

It started with us three;
Mike, LaVera and Me.

A game we'd played,
with words and saying
that had no relativity.

We'd say it loud and awkward,
No matter how it sounds.
We'd say it unconventionally
Regardless of who's around.

An explanation of Word Salad;
hearing rhythm, rhyme and pace.
But actual, Word Salad; the thought –
it goes all over the place.

W.S   And the rain never came down
to meet the ocean. And the ocean
never seen the sea. Because the
duck was slow – and the fish got
roe; and the four live in harmony.

86

W.S   But the mountains never catch
the sunlight. And the sunlight
never catch the stream. With
the temperature rising and snow
in the horizon; we're left with
a beautiful sunbeam.

W.S   Never came back to the sun,
cuz the river never seen the moon.
And the sky never touch the earth.
Earth and the stars in the sky –
Don't ask me why.
----- We call it Word Salad -----

Yeah, you just say whatever
come outta dat _____
That's right; say anything!

You see, it makes good sense to the three
------- Mike, LaVera and Me --------

Haven't Had Time to Pray

For those who kept up with the Jones –
Gaining homes and cars and titles that shown.
This expense of energy
        of effort
        on display,
I haven't had time to pray.

For those whose time is spent on matters –
Of other people lives on info you've gathered.
This quandary of gossip
        of meddling
        gone astray,
I haven't had time to pray.

To indulge in folly
        heresies
        and beguile
        haven't spent time on my knee's in a while.
        My home life in shambles, my soul is dismay,
I need this time to pray.

Vague Image

In the mirror I see a figment of a man
thirty years ago. However, I don't see
the man of today. I see me.

The age of my hair, I don't see. The
pounds around my waist; that ain't me.
The cognizant of who I am; position I
hold, all have its place. The bane of my
existence are an annoyance to this human
race.

You see, I brought with me a lifestyle of
lies and hypocrisy. Pathologically. I just
want, what I want – disregarding all policies.

This ganster-est; thuggishness life that
I knew – comes second nature of the things,
the things that I pursue.

Let me do it again – the same way I
did it back then. Using Russia, China

and Ukraine to assist me; My allies,
yes my friends.

I high-jacked this Grand Ole Party of
my chosen and its seems. I used corrupt-
ion as its mindset and the purpose of
this scheme.

In '16, out of 16, I was the middle man
in line. The ruler of dis MF (<u>expletive</u>) this
Republican Party is mine.

Liberty and Just-Us for All

*I pledge allegiance to the flag of the
United States of America. And to the
Republic for which it stands. One
Nation; under God; indivisible with
Liberty and Justice for all.*
Stop Lying !!!!

It all started with the seamstress, Betsy Ross.
Weaving the discord of injustice in the patterns
of red, white and what's **true.**

You see what's true is justice, in broader
terms means **Just-Us,** in the lighter form
of hue.

In our criminal system, is there justice
for all? Nah man. Just ask Governor Kay-
when she thought it was okay to lethally
inject our boy with her **just-us.**

The ruler ova "Bama", while she watched
him stamma, pledging allegiance to the flag.

All because she felt she had the goods on
Woods. When the trigger-man named Spencer,
vowed to convince her, that Woods was
grossly misunderstood.

A style of lynching done in a 2020 way.
Much like her predecessor 50 years ago;
happened on yesterday.

Her man Wallace, who had no solace for
the Black man or what he had to say.
"But I'm Innocent", nah Nigger. Not
in that black skin you portray.

Remnant of Our Past

We, collectively are a small of something even greater
than ourselves.

A small part of a greater whole, and is left with a
dream deferred.

Remnants, a form of cloth that's been worked into
a tapestry so the story of a people can live out their
identity; live out their creed.

And this tapestry with all its complexities are woven,
meshed and intertwined together; embellished with
varied colors and contrasting textures – that feel rough
early on and smooth as time passes. Passing on these
experiences and traditions to the strand of thread;
that we bring to this tapestry we call America –
all but to decorate some more.

When in need, our ancestral bond innately evoke and
summons those who has gone before us to give us aid.
Remnants is who we are and who we were.

We are the Remnant of Our Past

Bought with a price; and made to last.

Through trails our faith has been put to the task –

It's through God's grace we are the Remnant of Our Past.

I Got the Right

This is not a protest as in the 1955 Civil Rights movement
of Rosa Parks. Not the protest in 1965 stopping the Viet
Nam War.   No, this is a Temper Tantrum we started around
the Tea-Party in 2010; right on the USA front door.

In Minnesota, Michigan, Virginia, Maryland and even Ohio.
We're outraged at the Governor of Michigan for saying "not yet you
just can't go".

To work; to play; six feet apart, wear mask
and wear your gloves. What we want is the right to
demonstrate our feeling for what we love.

Our country back, and the way it was, but you're making
us stay at home. In Tantrum we are ignoring you with
our rallies and megaphones.

In the case of COVID-19 with, our economy all shut-up,
There is reporting of a man who says "I just want my
hair cut."

This abysmal thought of selfishness that I don't
want to see. The care for others safety means
nothing at all to me.

I Got the Right, to brandish my arms as the "Second
Amendment" has taught – I got the right and liberties
that our constitution has fought.

I Got the Right, to wave my flag in the Ole Confederate
way. To instill the fear and hatred that was born on
yesterday.

I Got the Right, to terror and kill, cloaked in white
supremacy. The right that I had brought from the
south is our cultural legacy.

I Got the Right, to follow a man whose agenda is
to divide – And lead this country to its knees; no
chance it will survive.

Those freedoms that we're entitled to despite the
fact I'm white. Goes all into the thought of me
I just have Got the Right.

He Ain't Raising No Hell

John Edward Thornton

He ain't raising no hell –

My father use to say.

He ain't raising no hell –

A slogan brought back from yesterday.

He ain't raising no hell –

This dude ain't making no trouble.

He ain't raising no hell –

Shawty can be found on the humble.

This is a phrase my father would often say. It basically meant that the person he was referring to wasn't making any trouble or they could be a push-over of sorts. Usually, my dad is in a relaxed state of mind when he'd make this kind of statement.

I'd often share his reflection with a few buddies of mine. We'd laugh at the generational divide, but the concept remained the same.

"He ain't raising no hell", *would be the same to say, "Oh, he don't mean no harm", or the proverbial Jill Scott song of "Gettin' in my Way" .... He's just a lightweight.*

BIDEN and the BUG

This prediction I see, with the help of Kamala, Amy or
Stacey. Is the ticket that restore this country's fate.
In addition to the fate is the germ that create a path
towards victory I'll be willing to debate.

BIDEN and the BUG, together they make the case
against this gangster, in (20), this thug. Together
binding (45); with the hydroxychloroquine drug.

With Biden, his compassion for folk, his foreign
policy gain. His knowledge of how government runs
on this he did campaign.

The Bug, of course we can't deny; is the source
of our concerns. The occupant in the house he's
frazzled; this matter he'd liked to adjourned.

But he cannot see the mere size and degree;
and the study of vir-o-logy. Not threaten of nick-names,
the commander of blame; of my genus and specificity.

I'll not be bullied; can't respond to tweets,

can't hear your political bluster. I'm COVID;

I'm not flesh and blood, your spiel is so lack-lustered.

Together they stand as a united front against

this POTUS- MAGA man. To restore our country

to what it was and not from which MAGA stands.

So Joe and COVID; Biden and the Bug are on

opposite sides of what wrong. To put our country

on its trajectory, not weak but to be made strong.

Glass Darkly

Although, it may appear;
But when seeing Him, face
to face, we shall behold Him
in His fullness.

The why, when and where?

And patience be my virtue.
Now sometimes I may falter;
but the overwhelming conscience
of Him … I line up.

Not liking those moments
that try men soul …
I line up.

Doing the things that makes
me common; and by nature
putting me at odds with them
who captures me ---- and they love it.
Let freedom ring – Not!
For those who have the keys
of the caged bird that sings.

Cuz; without the blood – there go I

Without the blood – make me ordinary,

prone to disaster.

Without the blood – don't have balance

and can't find my way.

Stuck in the muck and mire –

With those antecedent folk;

who live in glass houses …. Without the blood.

So I see through glass darkly

in my patience and when I falter.

And the good and the bad. And when I am

common. That one day I will be like Him.

And see Him for who He is.

Kitchen in Disarray

The walls are of grease and stained
The cabinets are thought to be aged.
The floor, that's linoleum –
would need a custodian,
less likely to appear to engage.

The sink not presently working.
The faucets in need of repair.
The cold knob dispense water –
that's all there is to offer,
the hot knob can't even compare.

The oven is in shamble, too
My cooktop cannot be replaced.
The burners are out dated-
they can't be replicated,
and Thanksgiving is postponed
at my place.

I have vision of a kitchen to be
Open concept to be able to see.

102

With countertops, crystal white-
island base of graphite,
my vision of concept and galley.

The flooring in white oak.
An effort to promote.
Uniformity will someway inspire-
openness is my desire,
a vision of style to invoke.

He Gave Me One Other

It was His design that they have two. He could

have made us with four, no five, though asymmetrically

I can't figure out why, but my mind is not the mind

of His; so He made two.

Two hands to shape a snow ball. Two hands to embrace

and hold. Two hands that play the piano so soft; as

in sound pianissimo.

Tragically I had suffered a stroke sixteen years ago.

And in that time I'd lost my ability to use my right hand –

Walking with a limp; kinda like a pimp, but with *One*

Other I was able to stand.

So I found a way to get around with my stroke.

I found a way to hang in with some hope.

With pencil in hand, and the writing began

With my left hand I seem to develop.

Sixteen years ago, the therapy at writing my first

check become a challenge. Forming letters,

legibly, was a difficult one to balance. But at
fortunes fate, it was mine to create a work
of art undisputed and unchallenged.

Keep This Quiet

After all I did for this family
You want me to keep this quiet?

Now I am good for following directions.
For listening to my elders.

For protocol and brevity.
For knowing what to say;
and what not to say.

While some work their havoc –
Just keeping things going.
Bad decisions made because of
preconceived ideas.

Missing out on opportunities,
because you got things wrong—
and so you suffer; in search for
a body who could share in your
own contrived dilemma.

One philosophical thought:
"Misery loves company"

At odds with other people,
having the rest of us sworn
to secrecy while you hold all
the cards.

"Keep This Quiet"!
Aiight ... I'll hold it.

But you know, *"Sunlight is the
Perfect Antiseptic"* to all things.
Just like prophecy _____
It all comes with time.

So be not concern with the
former things that would arouse
you to say something you don't
want to be repeated.

In thought, of one ____
who tells another that would
leave you so heated.

Aiight ......

Intuition

John E. Thornton

Off to college at 28. I considered myself to be a
late bloomer.
Bags were packed. Books were stacked; from
Annapolis to Atlanta in search for a better life for me.
I had made my mind that medicine, though challenging
a Biology Pre-Med major degree.

Morehouse College was my school of choice, of course
Howard and Fisk in view; but Morehouse held my
attention, the chartered course to pursue.

It was moving day. My mom; my buddy Michael,
seeing me off to school. Endearing hugs and kisses
reminded me of the days of pre-school.

Now just before the airport my father came outside.
With an all familiar bag it seems; the bag of my supplies.
My bag of clippers, curling iron; my scissors, combs
and sheets. My dad placed it in my hands stating,
"you'll never know what you meet."

"But dad I'll be studying medicine, no need of
these barbering tools. It's embarrassing for me
to be seen carrying these things to Morehouse
I'd feel like a fool.

But these tools were my salvation, my lifeline
and my help. One's prodigy my dad could see
it takes time to develop.

I'd thought about the women, and the men hair
that I did. Just recently; just hours ago my con-
science to forbid. I thought about this stand-off
between my dad and my will. What change my
mind, he told me, son you got some skills.

I took with me a legacy - of barbering and of style.
I brought with me the knowledge of how to make
my customers smile.

My foot touch-down, on Morehouse grounds at
Graves Hall my freshmen year. This is where
I start to pursue, my eight years of medical career.

November my curl had changed its course;
"new growth" begin to come through. I looked
around at the guys in-town and this style was
not what most were into.

No stranger to this, I begin to assist, my haircut
when all the while. A shout cried out, "That's
Thornton, no doubt", sound of clippers had
brought on a smile.

I'd charge $2.00 a head. My price, we're all
students with no "bread." As I looked around;
clientele was found of numbers close to one
hundred.

The money I made; I was able to pay the balance
of a tuition in full. At 33 years old, I did what I was
told and acted very responsible.

So the intuition of the man was right.
Who evoked a thought to insight
His decision was right, his acuity gave sight.
To a matter of intuition that I write.

Man from Minnesota

I'm a man that's from 10,000 Lakes; misfortune is my destiny.
A mid-western state that's way up north with southern taste
clandestinely.

From the state that borders Canada; far from the deepest
South. But men of my hue, regardless of my view is the thing
that this is about.

We're gathered like chattel, hunted like game they're dressed in the
traditional blue. Both hands on the wheel, comply when arrested
are the things that we go through.

Though handcuffed; and body goes limp, to show you're not
a threat. Regardless of the composure just our black lives is
the debt.

In prone position; face all down in dirty pavement deck.
One man in blue intentionally got his knee on my neck.
The others in blue secured me, while I lay there and
often frisked. They knew that shackled Blackman didn't

pose to them a risk.

I pleaded with him, as my life grows dim, and the

men I was underneath. Had thoughts to bequeath;

with mouth moving teeth and repeated man **I can't breathe.**

First minute, again I find myself in position of them who

gone before.

Second minute, will I escape the torture I care to explore.

Third minute, I heard the man said "get in the car," my

reply to him and the rest of them wasn't getting far.

Fourth minute, I wondered how some things could get bizarre;

living in this skin as black men that's just how things are.

Fifth minute, I envisioned my mother as I called

for her to come. I knew my life was ending and this

journey now was done.

Sixth minute, the life of me, as my limp body went cold.

The rest of that whole ordeal - is history as it's told.

Seven minutes ………………………………………

Eight minutes …………………………………………..

F o r t y…… S i x……S e c o n d s ……………

Jealous God

Exodus 34:14

He loves me

He loves me; not

He loves me

No pagan image

Nor worldly things –

Of home or car or wear on your back.

Or cake of crab;

to satisfy the flesh.

Appreciate … Not Gluttony

For these things have become your God.

And I'll not have that.

For I AM a jealous God

My New Living Room

It has all of the promise
of a comfortable, cozy, cabin.
With windows to see out of.
And a fireplace for warmth –
a room situated in the north –
with recess, in ceiling above.

It's a lovely room, adorn with a view
Of Marengo, in all that its use to.
Cars passing along –
The norm of a strong,
A strong neighborhood to raise
a family into.

This room of white oak; flooring to be –
Of spacious and tranquility
Walls of opaque and white –
With stairs 2 inches in height.
and the furnishing is grand and stately.

The Folks I Know

"I'm so glad we had this time together.
Just to have a laugh or sing a song.
Seems we just get started and before
you know it. Comes the time we have to
say so long." [1]

Cindy, Robin, Ramona, Porter
Beverly, Michael and Kim.
Were the creators of this tribute which
at Morehouse my freshman years began.

As saints they talked about church stuff;
remembering moments that passed. They
talked of individuals, and memories which
seemed to last.

To start with Mother Gray, of parables she'd often
adopt. That King Kids, lost and gone astray –
they'd never-ever eat slop.

Mother Dickerson warned the youth about the
dangers of herpes. Her understandings of STI's
wasn't Zeus but the god called Hercules.

Hadn't heard from me; where could he be,
at Spelman places I roamed. It's Robin request –
like Spielberg suggest of E.T. please phone home.

Alas the group get serious. As Ramona calls for
prayer. There's giggling, snickering and laughter
and such, no room for a prayer to be shared.

But Ramona calls; "In the Spirit" and commands
the essence at will. She would not begin; til her
party sees then and demands that peace be still.

---

1.   Carol Burnett; The Carole Burnett Show 1970's

Ostracized

I'm not a figment of my imagination knowing all too well
my surroundings.

You see I am **not** the self-conscience brother who feels
something growing out of the side of myself.
That psychosis-neurosis is foreign to me.
Nah, I base my thoughts on things logically.

Stripped from a place that embodies all the things
I hold to be true; of memories indelibly on the
mind, imbued.

Banded from the social functions that characterizes
a belongingness of shared values and norms. Extracted
from familiar sets where I was not informed.

Could we talk about some things that I had allegedly
done? Or mirrored acts or deeds by some; are as
equally shunned.

Hypocrisy 4.0

We, the most common of folk trying to get a handle of those things told to us. Dishearten and disillusion by what we see up above our heads. I mean we strive to get that piece of the pie, but the crumbs is all that we get.

Truth, justice and fairness seems to be a far-off object like a dream deferred. Never obtainable to the common kind. But our hope is built on nothing less as we try to fulfill on some happiness.

Our cry is one of **hypocrisy**. What's for me you see, ain't possible for the likes of you that we could on anything agree. Yeah, what's meant for you doesn't mean it's meant for me. Talking **hypocrisy.**

With the mail-in-vote, whether Kissimmee, Tallahassee or Miami. Your vote is marked coming from Washington, DC. But the **hypocrisy** is what you tout of voter fraud is linked with illegitimacy.

The mail-in vote is to protect the society.

Having our democracy; or protecting our safety

From corona-that we can break-free.

You see it's all about November 2020.

Washington, Colorado and Utah for the last past 20

years. They've voted by mail and such, no case of

fraud that U.S. needs to fear.

And in health care ……you congressmen and senators

have a good medical plan. But the common folk; this

administration seeks of Obama Care to be disband.

The latest is of panic, 'bout shielding us deaths of COVID.

But you've pushed the "panic" button 'bout black folks

coming where you live.

Hypocrisy, and lies and cheat, are the things you only

know. Unlike your GPA at Wharton – your "Hypocrisy"

is 4.0.

Lest Thou Forget

As early as 1441, the act of slavery had literally begun.

Portugal launched its seize on black bodies to oppress.
Was capital to gain and domination to their success.

Prince Henry contracted young Gonsalves –
West Africa the voyage was paved.
He took gold, spices and skins –
and helped himself to ten African slaves.

In benevolence this chattel was for Prince Henry –
In kindness the Prince shared with his Pope.
Pope blessed and sanctioned further expeditions
and the Africans were left for years without hope.

The precursor of the slave trade were the Portuguese.
Leading the rest of Europe for 100 years yet to be.
But the British who were innovators of the trade;
Made the slave trade into a specialized industry.

By eighteenth century the predators of this trade.

Using power and might, through slavery wealth was made.

Euro-America prosperity,

Using slavery that was free

The means and sufficient man power to achieve.

"Those who cannot learn history are doomed to repeat it." [1]

George Santayana

---

1. George Santayana; Philosopher

A Cough is Gonna Come

We are fearfully and wonderfully made.

God shaped and designed us unafraid.

But if something goes wrong,

That would do us great harm,

Our lives are in the balance; unsaved.

You just can't go throughout this life unscathed.

A Cough is Gonna Come

You germophobe; OCD; hypochondriac

A Cough is Gonna Come

This virus infested world; and the fear of being under attack

A Cough is Gonna Come

God has invested his protective immunity

A Cough is Gonna Come

To keep us safe from foreign agents we just don't see.

A Cough is Gonna Come

As mentioned in the word of God; dangers seen and unseen

The protection of our immunity is exactly what it means.

Anthrax, Tuberculosis, Rickets and the Pox

These agents of ruin take days to detox.

Pneumonia, mumps, measles and rubella
Meningitis, pertussis, tetanus – varicella.

Croup, herpes, tonsillitis and polio
Typhoid, strep throat and impetigo.

So in 40, 50 and 60 years in avoidance that you make.
The extended years; of weaken immune, the place it's
going to take.

Diabetes, Crohn's and Hypertension at the minimum.
Just remember with age, and toils of life, a cough is
gonna come.

We Signed Our Names

------------------ 1619 ------------------

Four hundred years ago we arrive to these
Virginia shores. As the descendants of the
1619 Projects.

Slavery, Europe's most vicious attack on people
of color. No greater act of violence in the annals
of history speaks of the dehumanization of one
      race over another.

And the name we signed were given by design.

Cultural and physical genocidal attempts were
made against the descendants of Africa.

The uprooting of kin and the raping of our woman
folk are just few of many painful moments we have
experience in Europe's quest to oppress people
of color.

And the name we signed were given by design.

Slowly but surely the conscience of Europe grew callous. The greater the purse of capitalism; the lesser the sensitivity to oppress. The greater the demand for productivity; the smaller were the concerns for cheap labor.

In the name of capitalism, *"she spoke lies of hypocrisy, having her conscience seared with a hot iron."*

Under the guise of Christianity Europe soothed her mind, making the unlawful acts of theft, murder and the bearing of false witness as an acceptable and justifiable means of religious recompense.
And the name we signed were given by design.

Boarded by the hundreds, packed like sardines were vestiges of families thrown together from every tribe and clan, no space in-between.

They spoke with other tongues, placed intentionally to be among; a tribe or clan not to communicate during this darken voyage, the old and the young.

On the Atlantic, the lost children of Africa became
the new fixtures of an old, cold, damp and dark ship.

Our shackled ancestors experienced all the gore
of rotting and diseased flesh; the sounds and smells
of dying men and women. All of the comforts a slave
ship had to offer.

The first being rum, made in New England was given
in exchange for African slaves. Some slaves were
returned – sold in the West Indies – in exchange for
cheap molasses.

Molasses was brought back to New England for the
distillation of more rum. And more rum was made
with the intent of continuing these triangular trades
and the intoxication of white people.
And the names we signed were given by design.

It's Better to Have Not Loved at All

For the years spent forming relationships only to have
them discarded and no warning or clue as to what I've
done.
You got me analyzing my days like a liar caught in his
tracks.
Checking my steps; hyperventilating, like a brother
having a heart-attack.
Trying hard to communicate and to established what
went wrong; with heartfelt feelings that are shunned and
so often prolonged.

It's Better to Have Not Loved at All

So one day I followed the advice of an old gospel song
 "I gave it over to the Lord and He worked it out"
A man a faith, I can forgive once a contrite heart is
exposed.

But years and years of self-aggrandizing and you
no longer holding the cards with my regards.

I asked you for something this bleeding heart
brings. HOW, WHERE and the WHO; the acts of purging?
Met with arrogant epic of "my deeds are done"
I only ask for a little transparency of how information
conceived was finally won.

Repeatedly, I'm a man of faith, and forgiveness
isn't a lost. But repentance; for all its worth do come
with a cost.

It's cool if you can't "jump that fence", don't
want to "climb that wall". It just makes sense
to act in defense; *It's Better to Have Not Love at All.*

White Bread

Like my daddy would say, "right now you eating
your white bread. What that mean? It means
you have the privilege to survive under the
shelter that I provide.

This food, clothes, gas and electric. Your room
and board the plug in the wall for you to be connected.

The light you leave on; Bruce, man that cost
money. I'm talkin' 'bout white bread, I know
you think that funny.

Ain't nothing free. You gotta pay something
wherever you go. You pay rent or mortgage;
whether here or Chicago.

And that water you got running – BRUCE;
cut it out. All you doing is brushing your teeth.
You ain't providing all the water in a lake
for a trout.

And once in a while, could you wash the dishes.
This ain't no restaurant, Bed-n-Breakfast or
hotel dismisses; all the thoughts you have in your
head, about the lap of luxuries of being cater to
mislead. Time and time keep telling you but ain't
nothing you gone get free. This the last time Imma
tell you; you eating your white bread.

Life Goal Post

We're both on different life trajectory.

Me going north,

You undoubtedly, trying to catch me.

I've sought the Lord for the call on my life.

You've sought my life –

No guidance, causing you much strife.

It's My Goal Post!

Not trying to move it close or far from you.

My goal post, be not concern for the things

I inextricably do.

Show Me Some Signs

In my attempt to understand the minutiae of medicine
Anatomy & Physiology was inevitable for me to accomplish.
Microbiology and Medical Terminology was mine to astonish.

I'd suffered a stroke some years ago. The anatomy is
in-tack, I questioned the physiology, I mean my nerves
there's no synapse.

The functioning is physiology, that's the part I can't explain.
The anatomy is it's structure all the part I still maintain.
When adjusting myself; and my alignment seems to shift.
It's the physiology and its properties that my body seems
to resist.

So show me some signs, I meditate, I anoint my body
with oil. Show me some signs that the physiology is
working so that my members don't recoil.

Tried acupuncture, physical therapy I prayed most night
and day. I prayed that this constrictor would cease and
you'd reshape this lump of clay.

Show me some signs, of how you'll change; restructure
these mortal limbs. And shape my life to what it was as whole
and vibrant again.

Show me some signs, that this COVID is really over. That I can
come out again. Some signs, that I'm not prone to exposure.

Show me some signs, when the masks leave our faces.
When sanitizing our hands; and leaving no known traces.
 "Like cold cream applied to the face leaving not one trace;
no not one trace." [1]

---

1.   Jeanne Crowner; 1979, When Pentecost Was Fully Come

What to do with These Hands

What to do with these hands that God gave me for today.
To protect the innocent and shield vulnerable and pray the
devil away.

What to do with these hands, though idle and thoughtless
seek mischief along. Write a thesis, calculate numbers
that your mind can then grow strong.

What to do with these hands, in anger, to weapon who
made you mad. Hug the brothers unselfishly until mad
turns to glad.

What to do with these hands when truth; you cannot
handle with pride. To resist the slap of the tellers face
that shouldn't be applied.

What to do with these hands that COVID - is here and
seems to stay. Wash them before you eat and handle
your kids both night and day.

You Should Have Killed Me When You Had Me

My name is Jacob Blake. I'm not Trayvon Martin
Tamir Rice, Eric Garner. Not Michael Brown or
George Floyd, Breona Taylor, Freddie Gray. My
name is not Sandra Bland or Philando Castile,
Walter Scott or Amadou Diallo.

My difference is I bear testament to injustice
because I'm alive. They've taken their voices
from them, but I was able to survive.

Seven shots in my back, while holding my T-shirt,
intending for my demise.
But I'm still here speaking truth to power – against
the odds, to their surprise.

Like Clemanta Pinckney and the eight others killed
at Mother Emanuel in search. If more were in there
he'd killed them too; this Dylan Roth is so unchurched.

No God to rule his life such that his hate has blurred
his vision. That the lives were lost and the price he cost
was at best a hellish decision.
But with a praying mother and a vigilant father
my fate was Godly induced. Both parents lead
to the source, have now been introduced.

The devil in him, and the God in me, unmatched
like boy to man. That officer who tried to kill me -
no chance of doing it again.

I understand when God is there, no devil in hell
can stop Him. From taking the life from his creation
no matter how dim or grim.

So "You Should Have Killed Me When You Had Me",
this story for you to take. I'm the voice, not silenced
from your gun as in Jacob S. Blake.